SPIRITUAL
PRICE TAGS

Your spiritual network determines
your real net worth

BENARD OBICHIE

ISBN: 978-1-7368215-7-2 (Paperback)

ISBN: 978-1-7368215-8-9 (EBook)

Published 2021.

Library of Congress Control Number: 2021918509

Cover Design by: DLX Press
Layout by: Kingdom Branding
Printed in the United States of America

Dedication

This book is wholeheartedly dedicated to God who saved me through His son Jesus Christ and empowered me with His Holy Spirit to be His mouthpiece. None of the pages of this book would have been a reality without the saving grace of God through our Lord Jesus Christ.

Furthermore, this book is also dedicated to my unequalled and darling wife Pastor Mrs. Dorothy Obichie and our wonderful children Light, Fruitful and Crown of Glory.

Table of Contents

Endorsements

Pastor Benard Obichie reminds the church of its true foundation in which lays her true power! Understanding Spiritual Price Tags will empower and equip the believer to live a victorious life through The Word of God! This book will challenge the believer to trust the work of Jesus Christ on the cross.

I would recommend Spiritual Price Tags as a great tool to instruct the Church of Jesus Christ in spiritual warfare and discipleship, as it is power packed with scripture. Pastor Benard Obichie is a rising leader for his generation and this book highlights the Hand of Jesus upon his life.

Hope you'll take time to purchase this book and encourage your circle of influence to do so as well. Understanding Spiritual Price Tags will strengthen and reinforce the believer's position in Christ!

His Servant,
Ted J. Howard Jr.
Pastor - Teacher
Edison Street Community Church

As I read through Spiritual Price Tags, I realized I had been led into a goldmine of knowledge, revelation, power, and wisdom.

The author, Pastor Benard, skillfully uses his power of communication to bring convergence to the doctrines of humanity and spirituality. Our lives are composed of our decisions and every decision has a price tag. Every decision we make is either taking us towards the destination we want or towards the destination we don't want.

However, the pain of the consequences of our bad decisions should motivate us to at least make better ones. But this is provided we are teachable. People who are unteachable are usually not impressed by the consequences of their bad decisions. As such, they tend to repeat the same mistakes; and each time they will have an excuse.

Benny clearly shows that there is a price for everything in life and that there's a spiritual price tag on everyone. He uses some tragic stories in the Bible to explain the mystery of spiritual price tags and spiritual dematerialization. The author rhetorically inquires why professing Christians seem to settle for less than Jesus paid for with His broken body and His shed blood. He provided a robust answer in his revelation about the threshold of blessing and the breaking of the spiritual glass ceiling.

The author vividly and graphically depicts the picture of a cursed anointing and what it means to be a lively stone. The message of the book is undeniable and you cannot read the book without a definitive understanding of who and whose you are vis-a-vis with your true value.

The urge to keep reading is all consuming. The book exemplifies knowledge and wisdom in moments of trial and temptation.

I commend this book without reservation and would encourage those who are thirsty for living water, on the journey of righteousness, to read the book and reread it at every milestone of challenges. The book contains treasures of empowerment for those who need to take control of their destiny. This definitely is a must-read and a must-keep book.

God bless!

Foluso Akinbola
Senior Pastor RCCG Chapel of Praise

This short and easy-to-read book will help you realize your true worth in Christ. Paradoxically it will also help you understand the high bounty placed on you by the devil to destroy the glorious future ordained for you by God. Until you realize how valuable you are, you will not be secured inside. People who don't know their true worth in God draw their value from seeking the approvals of men. They are never content nor secured in themselves. They draw fulfillment from what men say of them not what God has already made them—Waiting for its time of manifestation.

Benard has lucidly shown in this book how Satan readily exploits this ignorance of believers— "completeness in Christ" (Col. 2:10). Don't spend your life seeking the approval of men to enable you to get things that are already all yours from God (1Cor. 3:21). Live to please your Heavenly Father and do His will always without fear.

Kunle Omotoso
Continental Youth Coordinator, RCCG the Americas.

Foreword

This book has come at a time when professing believers now belittle the power of the blood of Jesus that purchased them. The reiteration of John 3:16 all along our faith journey will help reposition and dedicate us to take possession of all that God has for us. It is imperative that we understand the "Price Tag" God placed on redeeming us as children of the Most High. Understanding your Price Tag will stir up your spirit man to access ALL that God has provided for you in heavenly places.

Children of God, this book is a wake-up call! The devil knows your worth so he will stop at nothing to ensure he undermines and dematerializes your Price Tag. This is to stop you from accomplishing your God-given mandate here on earth. Spiritual Price Tags seeks to expose us to the weapon in the hands of the devil to reduce our worth. Proverbs 4:23 says, "Keep thy heart with all diligence; for out of it are the issues of life." The quality of our thoughts will determine the quality of life we live and how much value we are able to deliver. It is time to remove any barrier that limits the power of God in our lives or that prevents us from exercising our faith.

One of the ways we can continue to operate in the fullness of our Spiritual Price Tag is never to equate ourselves with the Master. Otherwise, our anointing becomes cursed or corrupted in a generation full of pride, hypocrisy, envy, etc. We are not called to make people like us but rather to be co-laborers with others that God has ordained. This book provides an understanding of John 3:16 to help us love people and work with each other. The best way to learn or cooperate with the Master Builder is to learn about leading while bleeding!

I strongly recommend that this book be read and used as a part of the Workers-in-Training manual in all parishes of The Redeemed Christian Church of God.

Yours in Christ,

Pastor (Dr.) James Fadel
Assistant General Overseer & Member of the Governing Council, RCCG Worldwide
Continental Overseer, RCCG The Americas

Acknowledgement

I would like to acknowledge God for His grace upon my life. No portion of this book would have been possible without His transformative power in my life. He is the reason this book made it to you.

I also want to give my warmest thanks to my lovely wife (Pastor Mrs. Dorothy Obichie) and my children for their support and sacrifice of countless hours of family time to assist me do what I do for the kingdom of God.

I sincerely appreciate all the fathers of faith in The Redeemed Christian Church of God and all over the body of Christ for their guidance and mentorship. I thank you all for your tutelage and continuous prayers.

I would also like to appreciate Moyofoluwa Aguda for painstakingly assisting in proofreading and constructive criticism. You have been a source of blessings to me and I want the whole world to know.

Finally, I appreciate the entire family of The Redeemed Christian Church of God, Fountain of Restoration Parish for their love and Support. The Lord Almighty bless you all beyond measure in Jesus mighty name.

Introduction

The world is a place of trade by barter. There is a price for everything—nothing is free, everything comes with a price. There is a spiritual Price tag on everyone, and these "Price tags" help us to understand who and whose we are. Moreover, with the said price tags, we can identify our worth—It is an invincible tag that portrays our true value.

This book is a powerful revelation that exposes the spiritual bounty the devil has on every believer in Christ Jesus. The enemy takes advantage of our human weaknesses to promote his evil works and distract us from our God-given destiny.

My desire is to help everyone understand what it means to be truly bought with a price (1 Corinthians 6:20) and to also unravel the bounty upon us.

Join me on the journey of knowledge and freedom.
Be blessed.

Benard Obichie

Chapter 1

Recognizing the Magnitude of Your Purchase Price in Christ Jesus

As a young child in my Sunday school class, I was taught our anchor scripture John 3:16 which reads, "For God so loved the world that he gave his one and only Son, that whoever believes in him shall not perish but have eternal life."

Whether a believer or not, you have heard this verse. The commonality and simplicity of this scripture have often prevented many from appreciating the benefit it offers to all. You may be reading this book and second-guessing God's love for you due to your sin. But I urge you to stop and think. The Bible says, for God so loved the world—That even in its sinful state He gave His only begotten son to pay the price of redemption for you and me. Regardless, if you believe in Christ Jesus or not, you are still valuable to God.

Perhaps the concept may seem ludicrous! Believe me, I also did not understand the efficacy of John 3:16, even with my familiarity with the verse. That was until God began to take me on the journey of spiritual trade by barter, also known as the "Spiritual Price Tag."

You see, there is no other way Christians could have been brought over to the kingdom of Light, had there not been a sacred transaction.

According to Colossians 1:13-14, "He hath delivered us from the power of darkness, and hath translated us into the Kingdom of His dear Son, in whom we have redemption through His blood, even the forgiveness of sins." In essence, the blood of Jesus was the only pleasing sacrifice to secure the freedom of mankind— Hence the "Spiritual Price Tag."

The sacred sacrifice offered us a once-in-a-lifetime opportunity of atonement (Hebrews 10:10), never to be repeated or sustained by any form of religious ritual of different sorts.

That blood (the blood of Jesus) still speaks today, as it did more than two thousand years ago (Hebrews 12: 22-24). If you recall in the Bible, Abel's blood called for vengeance, whereas the blood of Jesus delivered restoration (Romans 3:23). Jesus Christ paid a huge price to secure our stolen identity. The price tag hanging around our necks was "the blood of the righteous." 2 Corinthians 5:21 states, "He that knew no sin was made sin for us that we may become the righteousness of God in Christ Jesus." Truly, there was no other way to bargain man's freedom than with the blood of the lamb. As simple as this mystery may sound, you would be amazed to know that many professing Christians are not maximizing the power of the price Christ paid to secure our liberty because they do not place a demand.

Cultural, environmental, and religious factors have contributed to professing Christians not placing a demand on what had been made available to them in the kingdom. So many have been taught to be humble to a fault; some even have the notion that claiming the promises of God for your life is an act of arrogance. However, it is time you begin to engage the promises of God. Jesus Christ paid the price, so you need not fear. His redeeming love is the key to your future endeavors.

Speaking of engaging these promises, how do I go about that? Let's take a look at Matthew 11:28-30, "Come unto me, all ye that labor and are heavily laden, and I will give you rest. Take my yoke upon you and learn of me; for I am meek and lowly in heart, and ye shall find rest unto your souls. For my yoke is easy and my burden is light." The call to salvation is a call to discovering what is available to you in God's kingdom. You must discover your true identity by learning God's word (The Bible) daily and when you are of mature age (spiritual age), then certain treasures will be delivered for your manifestation.

Galatians 4:1-3 says "What I am saying is that as long as an heir is underage, he is no different from a slave, although he owns the whole estate. The heir is subject to guardians and trustees until the time set by his father. So also, when we were underage, we were in slavery under the elemental spiritual forces of the world."

Please remember the phrase, "even so we, when we were children, were in bondage under the element of the world" (Galatians 4:3). Christ paid a huge price for professing Christians not to remain "children" because children would always remain under tutors and governors, which may include unbelieving tutors and governors. Unfortunately, many professing believers still carry the child-like mindset—Therefore, limiting their ability to obtain the key to God's divine plan for their life.

Believers, your identity re-assures you of who is in charge! In Matthew 6:24-34, Jesus started by saying that you cannot belong to two masters.

Then He proceeded to say that if you belong to God, you should not allow worry to be your stay, rather you should be assured that God has got your back! Instead, seek first the kingdom of God and His righteousness and every other thing shall be added. Remember these things had been paid for even before you arrived at the scene of life, glory!

Your allegiance to God strengthens the affirmation of your identity and engaging all that has been provided for professing Christians. Do you know the world is waiting to hear your story on how much the gospel of Christ has impacted your life? Start by building your confidence in who you are in Christ Jesus, laying claim to the purchased price. Remember, you were bought with a price!

Let's go a little deeper in recognizing the magnitude of our purchased price as professing Christians. Jesus did not just guarantee us a worry-free tomorrow (Romans 8:28). Being worry-free does not mean you would be immune from the challenges of life, but it means God will make everything work together for your good. He guarantees a future that is ordered by Him as long as you are addicted to being available for Kingdom expansion. Don't forget the phrase, "but seek you first His kingdom and His righteousness." This implies that you should take advantage of the purchase price to partner with God for the expansion of His kingdom here on earth.

Psalm 16:5-6; "The Lord is the portion of mine inheritance and of my cup: thou maintaineth my lot. The lines have fallen unto me in pleasant places; yea, I have a good heritage."

The scripture above shows that God is interested in your tomorrow. He maintains your destiny (for true believers in Christ), meaning he orders the cause of your life right, even when it looks like things are not going the way you want it to go. Never forget, the way of man is not the way of God (Isaiah 55:8-9).

The purchased price gives professing believers access to inspiration. Your future is safe and promising. Apostle John declared "But the anointing you have received of Him abideth in you and ye need not that any man teach you: but as the same anointing teacheth you of all things, and is truth, and is no lie, and even as it hath taught you, ye shall abide in Him". Job 32:8 referred to this inspiration as the Spirit in man. Professing believers are well-positioned for life and Godliness due to the magnitude of the purchase price. You have what it takes! The price paid has given you access, it's up to you to obtain it and make use of it.

As a child, I remember always being afraid of what tomorrow would bring. This fear made me over-eat whenever we had a surplus at home, thinking I could hold a little more in my stomach for the next day, should there be no food to eat. My thoughts were like "Benard, eat a little more, be full now and make provision for tomorrow." It was not just with food—I gradually began to see the same thought process transcend into other areas of my life. I made impractical decisions based on limited understanding (which would spiritually equate to the limited revelation of God).

When I encountered God by the light of His word, I practically acted on every new revelation I received. This changed my perspective about life and introduced me to sufficiency in Christ Jesus. Many Christians are just like the elder brother of the prodigal son in Luke 15:31, "And the father said to him, you are always with me, and all that is mine is thine." There is abundance in the Kingdom we belong to (God's kingdom), but can only be engaged through revelation, and revelation is attained through study. You have been bought with a price, your future is guaranteed in the finished work of Christ on the cross of Calvary, however, you recover by revelation. You are holding this very book in your hand because you are in search of revelation. I urge you to go deeper, don't stop in chapter one, go deeper and discover the treasure the Lord has in store for you.

I challenge you to engage all the promises of God for your life by learning to recognize your place in Christ Jesus, maximizing the benefits of the speaking blood of Jesus, making yourself available for Kingdom expansion which guarantees a future that is controlled by God. The price has been paid. Recognize the sacrifice. Know that your worth is based on the finish work of Christ. This is your true identity so go forth and manifest.

Chapter 2

The Mystery of Spiritual Price Tag

The use of currency or barter as a medium of exchange is also applicable in the realm of the spirit. Jesus had to pay a huge price by shedding His blood as a medium of securing the liberty of those that truly believe in Him. In the same vein, Satan also has a measure of exchange called the "satanic price tag." The enemy knows how much everyone is worth in the realm of the spirit and is willing to do anything to derail those that are populating the Kingdom of God.

The devil has a spiritual bounty on every true child of God that is interested in seeing the Kingdom of God come through them. What do I mean? The devil is an unclean spirit and works with a network of other demons and these demons need human beings to operate.

In the case of Samson, the devil had to use the lords of the Philistines through Delilah to derail Samson from his God-ordained destiny (Judges 16:5).

A bounty was placed on Samson's life, an enticing one for that matter to bring Samson down to the path of destruction.

"And the lords of the Philistines came up unto Delilah and said unto her, Entice Samson and see wherein his great strength lieth, and by what means we may prevail against him, that we may bind him to afflict him and we will give thee every one of us eleven hundred pieces of Silver." (Judges 16:5).

A further study shows that there were five lords of the Philistines (Judges 3:3), meaning Samson's price tag was placed at eleven hundred pieces of silver multiplied by five, which will be a total of five thousand five hundred pieces of silver. This was irresistible for Delilah not to enroll as an agent of a satanic price tag. Samson was a danger to the Philistines, remember he was born for this cause (Judges 13:5). The devil knew then and still knows now who the Kingdom expanders are. Believe me or read it yourself in scripture, the enemy will do anything to derail them from their God-given assignment by placing a spiritual price tag on them which are attractive to demons—Who in turn look for available human vessels to carry out the assignment.

Our Lord Jesus Christ, the savior of the world was not exempted from the satanic bounty. The devil had to use the same system that he had previously used to try to derail our Lord Jesus from fulfilling His God-ordained destiny but he did not know that he was invariably promoting the mandate. 1 Corinthians 2:8 talked about the ignorance of the rulers in promoting the fulfillment of the messiah's assignment in redeeming the world back to Christ.

The religious authority set Jesus' bounty at 30 pieces of silver and was accepted by one of His disciples by the name Judas Iscariot. This was a script written by the devil but had to look for ready minds by the religious leaders to act out the script. The same is playing out in the body of Christ today, so many people are making themselves available as tools for the devil to carry out his already written script. The Bible says be sober (1 Peter 5:8).

Ironically, the devil promised Jesus everything if he just bowed and worshiped him. But everything belonged to Jesus anyway...and Jesus knew this. Hence, he did not take the bait. Matthew 4:8-9 describes the encounter, "Again, the devil took Jesus up on an exceedingly high mountain and showed Him all the kingdoms of the world and their glory and said to Him, "All these things I will give you if you fall down and worship me."

But Jesus was already the king of glory and did not need the devil to emphasize who He was. He was only going through a season before His manifestation. Listen carefully, many believers fall into the trap of the Satanic price tag by trying to be what they already are but are not willing to wait for the right time to manifest. The craving to be known and powerful has led some ministers of the gospel into joining "supposedly powerful cults" for them to network with the who is who. However, what they do not realize is that you do not need any platform that the Lord wouldn't want you to operate in. You are already powerful and famous. You don't need any occultic or social groups to validate what you already are, it is a bait from the enemy, and you don't want to be lured out of the covering of God for your life. Christ already bought you with a price and would like you to blossom in Him.

I am not discarding the place and importance of mentorship. However, any mentorship that does not point you to Christ and makes you more like Christ is a trap from the enemy to steal what you already have. Apostle Paul echoed, "Imitate me just as I imitate Christ!"

Again, you are already powerful, you don't need any occult or social group to make you powerful in Christ Jesus! You are going through a process, don't break the process, allow

God to perfect His works in your life, so you can stay up. Remember, those that grow up stay up, but those that jump up will surely come down. Don't fall into the demonic temptation. God has equipped you and is constantly there to walk you through.

Furthermore, agents of satanic price tag are ready vessels that the devil uses to disrupt kingdom-oriented projects. As for Judas Iscariot, just like many Judases in the Church today, he was close to the Lord Jesus and had access to his itinerary but was still overcome by his greed and craving for power.

Like Judas, you too may know what it takes to be a Christian or even occupy positions in the Church but also be an agent of satanic price tag, by being a ready vessel in the hand of the enemy to carry out his evil mandate. So many anointings are going stale because people that were once used as vessels unto honor have switched sides and are now making themselves available as agents of the satanic price tag.

To qualify as a victim of a satanic price tag you must have allowed the little foxes to spoil your vine (Songs of Solomon 2:15). The devil thrives on weaknesses that are not brought to check. Jesus was not a victim because he had this testimony, "that the prince of this world cometh but he has nothing in me" (John 14:30). The devil did not have anything to exploit or a foothold in Jesus' life even though a bounty was placed on him.

Samson's case was the opposite. Samson on so many occasions had transgressed but did not know that Delilah would be his last. Proverbs 29:1, "He, that is being often reproved and hardened his neck, shall suddenly be destroyed without remedy." Samson, like so many people, took the bait of price tag and cut short his

God-given mandate.

The devil has not stopped using the same bait of satanic price tag. It could be generational incline if you allow it! For instance, I know someone whose father was notorious for womanizing, and he too found himself in the same boat. The only difference is that he claimed to be born again but would not open up his secret life to get the necessary counseling and prayer to be set free. Rather he lives the same life his father once lived even while heavily involved in church activities. Talk about a generational satanic spiritual price tag.

The Satanic spiritual price tag does not respect titles or positions in the church. The Bible says, "Neither give no place to the devil" (Ephesians 4:27). So many destinies are being eroded because professing Christians are living contrary to what they say they believe. The Satanic spiritual price tag is thriving because of hypocrisy!

Samson was born for a special purpose, but he did not have enough discipline to say no to those things that gave the enemy a foothold in his life. The Satanic price tag suppresses a person's true value and amplifies the negative traits so the devil can easily lay claim to the person's life as a lawful captive. Whatever your weakness, seek God. He knows you more than you know yourself and loves you the way you are. Simply turn from sin and seek repentance.

You are reading this book right now because God wants you to be aware of the devices of the enemy. The devil is out using agents of satanic price tag to implement his already written script.

God's admonition to you is to put on the whole armor of God (Ephesians 6:10-18). Yes, the whole armor not some.

Don't leave out the belt of truth. Yes, let God know what you are battling with. Don't be ashamed to tell God the generational traits you are struggling with. Go get the needed counseling and stop living under the guise of church activities.

There is freedom for all those that are willing to expose the activities of Satan. Jesus said, come unto me all you that labor and are heavily laden, and I will give you rest. Yes, rest from the satanic price tag. Glory to God!

Chapter 3

The Threshold of Blessings

The word "blessed" in Hebrew means, "Empowered to prosper and increase" (Genesis 1:28). From the Bible, you can tell that blessings are in levels. Isaac was said to be great until he became very great (Genesis 26:13).

Threshold according to the dictionary means, "The magnitude or intensity that must be exceeded for a certain reaction, result or condition to be manifested." Jesus paid the ultimate price for an unlimited blessing, but everyone determines the extent to which you receive from God.

The Bible also talks about the situation where a cloud needs to be filled to pour down rain. In the same way, there is also a season of cultivating blessings for the needed harvest to be attained. No farmer expects a harvest for what he did not plant. There is a seedtime and harvest time (Genesis 8:22).

Sowers sow their seed in seedtime while eaters eat their seed that ought to be cultivated for the next harvest. It takes a lot of discipline to set aside seeds for planting and be determined not to eat them.

Isaac did not just attain the realm of unlimited blessings, he sowed against all odds at God's instruction. He wanted to go with the popular opinion, but God said, stay in this land where I ask you to live. Even amid God telling Isaac to stay and sow in the land, he had oppositions that wouldn't allow him to have a well to irrigate his crop and cater for his livestock. However, Isaac kept digging until the Philistines stopped striving with him.

Remember the agents of the satanic price tag in Chapter 2, they would do anything to derail you from God's best for your life, but God's word should be your anchor. Put on the whole armor of God to stand! The devil is consistent in making sure you take the bait that can derail you, but you must do all to keep standing!

Many professing Christians are unlike Isaac. Amid oppositions, they would have questioned if God really spoke to them. If God spoke to me, why am I going through the numerous oppositions? Remember, God used Isaac's opposition to help him develop a "never say no" mentality. So, believers are tough due to what they have been through in life. David saw Goliath and he concluded, the same God that helped me with the lion and the bear will deliver me to you into my hands (1 Samuel 17:37).

So many professing Christians miss their blessings because they give up too easily although the bible says, "Let us not go weary while doing good for in due season you will reap if you do not lose hope" (Galatians 6:9). Your blessing has a threshold, meaning it must reach a certain magnitude to command results. Your mindset should be doing things as unto the Lord not unto man, then your reward will be guaranteed. I love the admonition that says, "do it as unto the lord and not unto men" (Collossians 3:23).

Many professing believers have cut off the flow of blessings because they allowed themselves to be overtaken by emotions, using logical conclusions as a means of giving or allowing themselves to be a blessing. Is it possible for God to allow you to serve where you would not be appreciated? 1 Peter 2:18 says, "Servants, be submissive to your masters with all reverence, not only to the good and gentle but also to the unreasonable." How could God ask you to be submissive and serve those that are unreasonable? Simple, because it is not about them but you. The principle of the threshold of blessings is applicable in all areas of life, at work, in your relationship with your spouse, friends, church leaders, and so on. Remember, you serve the Lord God. If God has placed you in their lives, rest assured that God knows who is just, so do not hold back in giving your best so you would not stand in the way of you getting to the threshold needed for blessings. Just look at Joseph who was treated unfairly and was in prison for the offense he did not commit, however, he did not stop being a vessel in God's hand even in the prison. He did not stop being sweet! Have you lost your sweetness due to your experience of betrayal and false accusation? It is a trap to deny you of the threshold of blessing, so pick yourself up from the confine of self-pity and condemnation, and declare that you are unstoppable.

Maybe you think people often use you to get what they want, yet you cannot resist helping them. The truth is that they are not using you, you are the one using them to get to your threshold. A lot of people have stopped being useful in the church because they feel used, not knowing that they are robbing themselves of a glorious future ahead. God is not unjust, if He keeps prompting you to do something against your will then there is a blessing attached to the assignment. Do not stop your threshold by refusing to serve the undeserving! Refuse to allow your emotion to get the best of you. 2 Timothy 2:6 says, "The husbandman that laboureth must be the first partaker of the fruits."

Your labor is unto the Lord and not unto anyone. God rewards, but does not reward everyone at the same time. You have not been forgotten. Don't stop the flow of the blessings. Your investment in the kingdom is not in vain.

So many believers have lost what they have gathered in the conduit of the threshold of blessings due to weariness and backsliding. Ezekiel 18:24 reminds us, "But when the righteous turneth away from his righteousness, and committeth iniquity, and doeth according to all the abominations that the wicked man doeth, shall he live? All his righteousness that he hath done shall not be mentioned: in his trespass that he hath trespassed and in his sin that he hath sinned, in them shall he die." Look at the phrase, "All his righteousness that he hath done shall not be mentioned (remembered)". Don't stop the flow of your blessings, you are on the right path to attaining the threshold of blessings!

I remember when I got into ministry. I carried out every assignment that was offered to me in the church, not to please anyone but as a lover of God. I could not stand to see the work of God at a standstill. I even offered to mow the church's lawn with my bare hands, because I understood the mystery of the threshold of blessings. No one gets to the top of life by accident, there is always a price to pay for every greatness that you want to attain in life.

In the kingdom of God, there are set principles that determine how far you can go in the kingdom. 2 Timothy 2:5 states, "And if a man strives for masteries, yet is not crowned, except he strives lawfully." The principle to moving from the realm of being blessed to being a blessing is attaining the threshold of blessings. You cannot just pray it into fruition, remember as believers when we pray God teaches us what to do to receive the manifestation of your prayer. You are always part of your answer prayer (1 Kings 17:8-16). Look at Elijah, he was nourished by the ravels and he drank from the brook until the brook dried up and Elijah cried to God. His answer came but he had to be part of the answer, by obeying God's instruction on this matter. "Get up and go to Zarephath in Sidon and live there. I have instructed a woman who lives there, a widow, to feed you."

If Elijah refused to arise and do just as God had said to him, he would not receive the manifestation of the answered prayer. Have you carried out the last instruction God gave to you or are you hell-bent that you cannot allow yourself to be belittled by the action God instructed you to carry out? You can be the one stopping your threshold from reaching breaking point to propel unlimited blessings. You may never get another instruction until you obey the last order. Maybe you have learned the religious way of trying to please God with rituals or activities, God is not the author of confusion, His word cannot be replaced. Obedience is better than sacrifice (1 Samuel 15:22).

The Bible talks about Cornelius' alm giving that got the attention of God. His testimony was that "thine alms come up for a memorial before God" (Act 10:4). Cornelius gave until his giving got to a threshold of blessings.

Cornelius was an example of a liberal soul that the Bible talks about in Proverbs 11:25, "The liberal soul shall be made fat and he that waters shall be watered also himself." The word liberal is not a political term as in liberal vs conservative, but it means a generous and thoughtful individual who adopts Jesus Christ as a model for treating other people. Cornelius' alm got God's attention because he did it unto the Lord. For you to get to the threshold of blessings, make sure that everything you do is done unto the Lord not unto any man.

There is a cloud of breakthrough for every professing believer according to Ecclesiastes 11:3. If that cloud is full of rain, there will be a shower of blessings.

The threshold of blessings also comes with a litmus test that needs to be attained to command the needed manifestation. A litmus test is a test that a single factor such as attitude, event, or fact is decisive in the attainment of the needed manifestation. The Bible encourages us to add virtue to our faith (2 Peter 1:5) because your attitude can greatly influence your output which will otherwise determine the threshold needed for certain blessings.

It is time for you to ask God, "how can I be of use to you?" Just as Paul the Apostle did after his conversion, we will accumulate real blessings that would in turn lead to showers of blessings.

Chapter 4

The Mystery of Spiritual Dematerialization

"Dematerialization in economics refers to the absolute or relative reduction in the quantity of the material required to serve economics functions in the society." In other words, it refers to the concept of doing more with fewer resources.

In the realm of the Spirit, there are two types of spiritual dematerialization, positive and negative.

Remember the lunatic man of Gadarenes (Mark 5:1-20)? As soon as Jesus got to the country of Gadarenes, he was met by this dematerialized man that later introduced himself as, "...legion-saying because we are many." The devil needed a territorial opposition to Jesus' ministry; he had to prepare that man, but when he (devil) failed, he then used the people of the land to force Jesus out of the land. Many people do not understand that the devil is always looking for ready vessels to use to accomplish his mission. Because his time is short, he does not use them for one purpose only, but for many! In the world of building construction, every building has a carrying capacity, just like humans we have a carrying capacity.

That is the reason why the foundation of a building is the most critical part of the building. It must be able to bear the load that would be placed on it. The devil uses spiritual dematerialization to gain more lives for his use by introducing different spirits. The Bible mentions that if an evil spirit leaves a man, he goes into the desert seeking rest but if he finds none, he will come back to the life he was previously cast out of and if it is suitable, he will go and look for seven other spirits more evil than himself to occupy (Matthew 12:43-45).

The devil introduces more spirits to destroy the carrying capacity and make the person lose his/her mind. If you see someone that is not medically challenged but has lost his mind, chances are the person is a victim of spiritual dematerialization. Professing believers must guard against making themselves available for use by the enemy because he never stops introducing more spirits that would make them lose their minds. According to Mark 5:15, "Then they came to Jesus and saw the one who had been demon-possessed and had the legion, sitting and clothed and in his right mind. And they were afraid."

I love the phrase, "in his right mind." That is what the devil does not want you to know, you need to guard your mind with all diligence (Proverbs 4:23). The quality of your mind would eventually determine the quality of your life. You can do this by consistently self-examining yourself. Jealousy does not stay by itself, it comes with other spirits, worry does not just stay by itself it comes with anxiety, nervous breakdown, and pessimism which could make you lose your mind.

Are you a warehouse where the devil stores his tools? Remember what Isaac told Esau after he had given the blessing to Jacob? He said the blessing is redeemable, but it is a choice that you need to make. Genesis 27:40 says, "...and it shall come to pass when thou shall have the dominion, thou shall break his yoke from off thy neck" meaning, you have to want it badly to get it.

If you have noticed any trace of consistent manifestation of the works of the flesh: Jealousy, envy, antagonism, backbiting, slandering, division, immorality, theft, bearing false witness etc., rest assured that there is more to them. The devil uses the tool of spiritual dematerialization to terminate people's callings. When the lunatic man of Gadarenes got to his right mind, he listened to the Lord Jesus and departed and began to proclaim in Decapolis all that Jesus had done for him and all marveled. (Mark 5:20) That was his true calling. He reached his potential when he was delivered of satanic dematerialization.

Furthermore, there is a positive spiritual dematerialization—The compressed blessings of God that take creative faith to bring into reality. When I was newly born again, I easily experienced the answer to prayer in a child-like manner that solidified my confidence that God truly exists. As I grew in faith, God started to teach me the principle of creative faith which brings compressed blessings of God into the realm of manifestation.

Ephesians 1:3 states, "Blessed be the God and father of our Lord Jesus Christ, who hath blessed us with all spiritual blessings in heavenly places in Christ." The word all spiritual blessings translate to all you need for life. Carefully examine 2 Peter 1:3, "According as His divine power has given to us all things that pertain to life and godliness, through the knowledge of Him who has called us to glory and virtue."

It is clear that God had prepared dematerialized blessings in the knowledge of Him; however, you determine if these dematerialized blessings will manifest.

All blessings come in the form of secrets that need to be unraveled by a spiritual person. 1 Corinthians 2:14 states, "But the natural man receives not the things of the spirit of God; for they are foolish to him; neither can he know them because they are spiritually discerned." The point made in this verse is crucial in our understanding of spirituality and how to interact with the non-believing world. The key difference between a believer in Christ and a non-believer is not intellect, morals, reason, or evidence, but that believers are guided by the Holy Spirit to locate the dematerialized blessings. The Holy Spirit gives believers a spiritual perspective on how to get the blessings that God has in store for them.

The non-believer rejects any leading that comes from the spirit of God; they use their human senses while believers are propelled by the Holy Spirit.

It is possible to get a glimpse of what God has in store, but your obedience will determine if you maximize these treasures. Many believers started out being meek/leadable but when they ascended the ladder of greatness, it became so difficult to lead them. A case in point was Uzziah. The Bible has a testimony of him as follows, "But when Uzziah was strong his heart was lifted to his destruction for he transgressed against the Lord his God by entering the temple of the Lord to burn incense on the altar of incense" (2 Chron 26:16). Uzziah started by being meek but thought he had gotten to the apex of God's blessings for his life and his heart was lifted against God. This passage applies to many believers' lives, not knowing that there is more for believers that would allow God to continue to lead them and they would obey no matter what level they have attained.

The Bible further alluded, "The meek would He teach His way" (Psalm 25:9). Let the Lord guide and teach you how to maximize the blessings of sonship. There is more to God than you ever imagine, please don't settle for less. So many believers are like the widow of the prophet that served Elisha in 2 Kings 4:1-7. She had the solution to her problem at home in dematerialized form but was not aware until the man of God spoke the needed word into her life. We all have latent abilities, yet we still need the right word to breathe upon our potential.

We must continue to seek grace and not to be spiritually myopic or opportunity-blind. Just as we have people that are color blind, we have believers that are opportunity blind. The scripture alluded to this in Proverbs 20:12, "The hearing ear and the seeing eye, the Lord has made both of them." To recognize blessings in their dematerialized state requires a hearing hear and seeing eye. They both belong to the Lord, so you can continue to engage God for these unusual gifts, then you would be exceptional in all you do. We can all operate at a high level, yet we must gain the insight and become wholeheartedly willing to abide in Christ. John 15:4 reminds us, "Abide in me, and I in you. As the branch cannot bear fruit of itself, except it abide in the vine, no more can you, except you abide in me."

There is no time for playing games, if you want to access everything in Christ you have to be consistent and go deeper in Him.

Chapter 5

Breaking the Weight of Spiritual Glass Ceiling

The dictionary defines the glass ceiling as, "an unofficially acknowledged barrier to advancement in a profession, especially affecting women and minority groups."

A spiritual glass ceiling is an invincible barrier that prevents people from attaining the success they see others around them achieving. They often try but just seem to bounce off this invisible barrier. If professing believers want to reach their full potential, they must realize that the mystery of the glass ceiling is real and needs to be dealt with.

Part of the price Jesus paid for professing Christians is for them to break limits. In Christ Jesus, there is no room for settling for less or maintaining the status quo. Ephesians 3:20 helps us understand that God's plan for us does not have a glass ceiling, and His promises are always exceedingly and abundantly more than we could ever imagine, nevertheless these glass ceilings exist.

It is possible to be destined for greatness but if you do not engage the principles that make a prophecy a reality, one can die a nobody.

Jabez in 1 Chronicles 4: 9-10, was more respected in his family. There was a mark of honor on him, but he was suffering from the weight of the glass ceiling placed on him by the pronunciation of his mother. Jabez carried that weight even though he was serving God until he admitted that he needed divine intervention. Living in self-denial does not help in any way to reduce the impact of the weight of the glass ceiling. You must identify what the problem is and give it a name, then you can use the name of Jesus to address such a weight. Jabez knew he was not living the life people were attributing to him, he was held in high regard but was limited by the weight of the glass ceiling. Philippians 2:10-11 begins with, "And Jabez called on the God of Israel saying, Oh that You would bless me indeed, and enlarge my coast, that Your Hand would be with me, and that You would keep me from evil, that I may not cause pain. So, God granted him what he requested."

I love the phrase, "that you would bless me indeed." It is possible that people think you are blessed, but you know you are drowning under the weight of a glass ceiling. Jabez was not pretending, he was up-front with God about the situation. Are you up-front with God regarding your limitations or are you hiding under the guise of religion and activities? Jabez got the answer to his prayer because he was real with God.

Another interesting thing Jabez did was that he decided it was time for a breakthrough. He put all his eggs in God's basket, he did not have an alternative. He took the matter to God in prayer and stayed put until he got the needed breakthrough. You can decide that it is time for a breakthrough on the authority of God's word. Luke 18:7-9 says, "Shall God not avenge His elect who cry to Him day and night." You are God's elect, let Him hear you talk to Him as a father to son relationship, not a slave to master relationship.

Jabez also went ahead to place demands that would cancel the burden of the glass ceiling that he was going through and his demands were granted. A lot of people are aware of the pain of the glass ceiling they are going through but have never taken the bull by the horn to place a demand on manifestation that would delete such a burden. You would need to place a demand and test the manifestation by daring things you would not have done and going to unfamiliar territories and trusting that God would come through for you.

Glass ceilings could be generational as in the case of the sons of Rechabites (Jeremiah 35:2-10). Though their father had good intentions by asking them not to drink wine, he also asked them to dwell in tents, not to plant vineyards nor have them that there may be many in the land.

The glass ceiling placed on them by their father was generational because they did not only practice it, they also intended to pass it on to their generation when they passed on. This household would never attain generational wealth which is God's desire for all professing believers. So many people are tied down by generational glass ceilings because they still believe in culture, tradition, and religious rituals which is contrary to what the word of God says.

I once spoke to someone who claims to be a professing believer but forbids certain foods, not due to health challenges or a doctor's recommendation. His reason is simply that it is forbidden by his father's house. Christians cannot cherry pick God's instructions, it is either you are in or out. There is nothing like sitting on the fence. Remember, you are a servant to whom you obey (Romans 6:16). The sons of Rechabites were held bound by their father's erroneous belief that denied them access to what they could have attained in life. Your belief system is where the negative glass ceiling thrives. Do you still have things that you firmly believe are not biblical?

I have met a Christian who believes fellow Christians should not live in certain cities stereotyped as supposedly corrupt like California or Los Angeles. If a man with such belief grew in a family under a generational glass ceiling of stagnancy, he will continue to remain stagnant in some areas of his life that require him to live in California or Los Angeles for greater exposure and success. He has rejected opportunities that could have introduced him to the missing link of his life, not knowing that believers have been called to be gatekeepers, meaning God has repositioned every believer to carry out His mandate in your locality. Don't forget, it is not a place that makes or guarantees a person's salvation, but it is the people that make the place! The first set of believers influenced Antioch to the point that they were nicknamed Christians. You have what it takes to influence your city, you are the salt of the earth and the light of the world. However, you cannot conquer the glass ceiling with a victim mentality. You need to break the limiting thoughts for you to rise above the bench-mark.

Furthermore, some professing Christians have this erroneous belief that "not everyone should pray in tongues, more-so American Christians shouldn't be too spiritual, since we don't have a lot of spiritual forces compared to other third world countries." These notions are limiting thoughts that have ensnared a lot of believers. They have not been able to be fully built up because of these erroneous beliefs. Jude 1:20 says, "But you beloved, building yourself upon the holiest faith; praying in the Holy Spirit". The way up spiritually is to learn to pray in the Holy Spirit.

Ephesians 6:12, "For we wrestle not against flesh and blood, but against principalities, against powers, against the rulers of darkness of this world, against spiritual wickedness in high places." There is spiritual wickedness in high places in all nations of the world, America is not excluded. This spiritual wickedness has found a way to camouflage their activities, just as the scripture says, in 2 Corinthians 11:14, "And no marvel; for Satan himself is transformed into an angel of light." Don't allow yourself to be deceived by categorizing Christianity based on the comfort level of a country. A true believer is supposed to be on fire for God to break his bloodline glass ceiling and other environmental glass ceilings.

Remember, as a man thinketh so he is—To walk and live as Christ did in victory over glass ceilings, you must have the mind of Christ too. To successfully run the race that is set before you, you must shed every negative weight that can easily beset you either directly like sin or indirectly like unbiblical beliefs that promote glass ceilings.

Even though the spiritual glass ceiling is real and denies people access to maximizing their destinies, the energy and pressure it exacts should be resisted by operating in faith and not by sight (Romans 1:17). Do not look at the size of the obstacle but look at the size of the God who has the power to overcome the obstacle you are confronted by. God has called us into deliverance according to Colossians 1:13. God did not save us to remain under the element of this world. He has saved us to serve out His purpose, but we must engage these covenants. Remember, the glass ceiling will not be destroyed by your ability, its destruction lies in the authority in the name of Jesus. 1 John 5:4, "For whatever is born of God overcome the world. And this is the victory that overcomes the world, even our faith."

God has given us everything we need to destroy the spiritual glass ceiling in our lives.

He has given us His word (2 Timothy 3:16), He has given us His Holy Spirit (John 16:13), He has given us His precious promises (Proverbs 30:5). Glass ceilings do not stand a chance when we repel its attack with the tools given to us by our heavenly father.

The weight of the glass ceiling has limited so many believers from reaching their God-ordained destiny, which ought not to be since we are more than conquerors. Decide to call it by name, claim the promises in the written word of God for your life, and refuse to remain underwater.

Chapter 6

A Cursed Anointing

Maybe you are wondering, how can an anointing that is good be cursed? Is this not heresy? Please be patient as we embark on unraveling the mystery behind "A cursed anointing."

Ezekiel 28:13-16 says, "You were in Eden, the garden of God; Every precious stone was your covering; The sardius, topaz and diamond, Beryl, onyx, and jasper, Sapphire, turquoise, and emerald with gold. The workmanship of your timbrels and pipes was prepared for you on the day you were credited. You were the anointed cherub who covers: I established you: You were on the holy mountain of God; You walked back and forth in fiery stones. You were perfect in your ways from the day you were created, Till iniquity was found in you. By the abundance of your trading, you became filled with violence within and you sinned; Therefore I cast you as a profane thing out of the mountain of God; And I destroyed you, O covering cherub, From the midst of the fiery stones."

Lucifer, before he became the devil, was heavily anointed, but his anointing became cursed when iniquity was found in him. What kind of iniquity could make an anointing like Lucifer's to be cursed?

Lucifer was created by the creator, but became egocentric and saw himself as equal with his creator. The Bible recorded the account of this display in Isaiah 14:12-14, "How art thou fallen from heaven, O Lucifer, son of the morning! How art thou cut down to the ground, which didst weaken the nations! For thou has said in thine heart, I will ascend into heaven, I will exalt my throne above the stars of God; I will sit also upon the mount of the congregation, in the sides of the north. I will ascend above the heights of the clouds, I will be like the most high." Lucifer carried out the first rebellion in heaven and deceived some angels in carrying out this atrocious act. His anointing became polluted and cursed.

The trend of recruiting more physical bodies is still on. Satan, also known as Lucifer, has placed a tag on people and is also using their human weaknesses to lure them into his trap. Paul the Apostle was mightily used by God but the devil marked him, hence God had to use "a thorn in the flesh" to checkmate him so he would not be prey to the enemy's trap. 2 Corinthians 12:7 says "Because of the abundance of the revelations. Therefore, so that I might not become too elated, a thorn in the flesh was given to me, an angel of Satan, to beat me, to keep me from being too elated." Some believers fight the process with different Christian rituals, instead of allowing God to perfect the work that he has started in their lives. Believers must learn not to fight the process but cooperate with the workings of the Holy Spirit in their lives. "For It is God that works in us both to will and to do of His good pleasure" (Philippians 2:13).

God needs your absolute cooperation for you not to be a victim of the satanic price tag. So many believers are yet to understand that the way of God is different from the way of man. It takes a spiritually mature believer to see God even in situations that may seem tough, yet he can still sense the ever-abiding presence of God.

When this kind of trust occurs, we see God's delivering hands.

There are various reasons why a professing believer can start as a genuinely anointed servant of God but the same anointing can be corrupted along the way. The most common one is the craving for position and power. So many Believers forget that no matter the position they occupy, you serve the Lord God! (Colossians 3:24). As soon as you begin to rely solely on yourself as if you are the end-all be all, the devil takes a foothold and begins to corrupt your anointing. Our anointing is guaranteed freshness as long as it serves the master's purpose (God). Ecclesiastes 10:1 states, "Dead flies cause the ointment of the apothecary to send forth a stinking savor: so doth a little folly him that is in reputation for wisdom and honor." What are the habits or tendencies that represent dead flies in your life? Remember, your anointing can start up fresh, but if there are dead flies like pride, hypocrisy, envy, jealousy, tribalism, immorality, cravings for popularity and power and so on, you can count your anointing in danger.

You know when you are crossing the line. Samson did the same until he met his waterloo. He said to himself, "I will go out as at other times before and shake myself. And he wist not that the Lord was departed from him" (Judges 16:20). God is merciful but He is also a God of accountability. If He has given you much, much is expected of you! The anointing is for service not for personal gain or profiting. When a professing believer starts representing himself instead of the master, he outgrows God's usefulness and becomes a candidate for corrupt anointing.

As believers, we all grow on the shoulders of those that have gone ahead of us (Spiritual fathers). The specification for a spiritual father is not age, but the operation of the undeniable grace of God upon a person's life and the wisdom of the word of God. Paul admonished Timothy in 1 Timothy 5:17, "Let the elders that rule well be counted worthy of double honor, especially those who labor in the word and doctrine." I have heard some believers say, "we are all the same in Christ!" Yes, we were saved by the same blood that was shed but God is a God of order. We are not the same hierarchy in the realm of the Spirit, we operate in different grace and must appreciate what others have that we do not. So do not be jealous and entertain the root of bitterness which has corrupted a lot of people's anointing just like Lucifer's.

The Spirit of God does not strive. Where there is strife, it is flesh and not the anointing that is in operation. Lucifer lured one-third of the angels to strive so if you notice that you are prone to strife, even if you can justify the reason for striving, you may be heading down the path of cursed anointing. The Holy Spirit does not correct a wrong with a wrong method, God is the God of order. Don't promote strife in your life with the defense of correcting a wrong—It has led to a lot of people walking in cursed anointing, just like Lucifer did when he broke the order he once submitted to.

The Bible says in James 3:16, "For where envying and strife is, there is confusion and every evil work." Even the outcome of justifiable strife, no matter how good it looks, is considered "confusion and evil work." A lot of Christians, including ministers of the gospel, are going about with corrupt anointing (because of strife), which leads to confusion and evil works. God is not the author of confusion and evil work, the devil is.

When Godly orders are intentionally violated, it leads to misalignment in many aspects of life especially in our walk with God. People begin to hear the voice of their flesh rather than the Holy Spirit because they are not in alignment and thereby operate in Cursed anointing. I urge you to swallow your pride and listen to the voice of the Holy Spirit, you are a soldier of

50

Christ, and your life needs to obey the order of Christ to operate in His anointing.

Chapter 7

Called To Be Lively Stones

In the world of building and construction, there are different types of stones for different construction purposes. The quality of the stones used would, to a great extent, determine the strength of the building. That is the more reason the scripture is keen on foundation. "If the foundation be destroyed, what can the righteous do" (Psalm 11:3). In the new testament dispensation, Christ Jesus became our foundation and empowered us to be lively stones to carefully build for Him. 1 Corinthians 3:11-15 says, "For no other foundation can no man lay than that is laid, which is Jesus Christ. Now if any man builds upon this foundation gold, silver, precious stones, wood, hay, stubble; Every man's work shall be made manifest; for the day shall declare it, because it shall be revealed by fire; and the fire shall try every man's work of what sort it is. If any man's work abides which he has built thereupon, he shall receive a reward. If any man's work shall be burned, he shall suffer loss; but he himself shall be saved; yet so as by fire."

Professing believers and non-believers are different types of stones used for building different kingdoms. Christ paid the price for all professing believers to build for Him while on earth.

Mark 9:40 says, "For he that is not against us is on our side." Humans are building blocks with influence, depending on what side of the divide you are, your influence is being used for good or bad.

1 Peter 2:5 says, "You also are lively stones, are built up a spiritual house, a holy priesthood, to offer up spiritual sacrifices, acceptable to God by Jesus Christ." The word "lively" in Greek means Zoe or life. The Christian life is not just human existence but life in fullness as a result of the operation of the Holy Spirit in man. Simply put, it is the life of God. As clearly stated in John 10:10, "....that you may have life and have it more abundantly."

Lively stones entail the supernatural workings of the Holy Spirit in the lives of believers that enable them to build for God or carry out God's mandate on earth (making an impact for God). Some stones are not lively but dead because they can only be used for dead works as noted in Hebrew 6, "Therefore leaving the principles of the doctrines of Christ, let us go on unto perfection, not laying again the foundation of repentance from dead works, and of faith towards God." It is important to note that so many started as lively stones but they allow flesh to put out the fire in them, thereby making them dead stones. In the kingdom of God, there is no lone ranger, you have to work in partnership with other professing believers. 1 Corinthians 3:9-10 says, "For we are laborers together with God; you are God's husbandry, you are God's building. According to the grace of God which is given unto me, as a wise master builder, I have laid the foundation, and another builds thereon. But let every man take heed how he builds thereupon."

Being a lively stone is a teamwork with other professing Christians that you do not agree with on everything about life, but for the sake of the kingdom, there has to be trade-off to adequately build for God. So many have lost their ministry because their philosophy about life is not the same as their group members. God did not call us to make people like us, but He called us to be co-laborers with others that He has ordained us to work with. Some would rather give up their ministry instead of working with people that their philosophies about life do not tally with theirs. I will like to refer you to Paul's word, "as a wise master builder, I have laid the foundation, and another build thereon."

I remember almost giving up on ministry because of pressure from people that I have served and loved the best way I know how to. It was a painful season for me, yet the best moment of maturity. I learned about leading while bleeding! God wants to see your commitment to Him and not to others in building for Him. Have you left the real place God wants you to build. Remember you can't just decide where you build? I have heard so many believers leave a church that God wants them to stay put and build. Your co-laborer may not be the best, your first lady, pastor, deacon, deaconess may not have the same life's philosophy as you but if the word of God is everything that is used and applies in that gathering and God once told you to go and build with them, don't switch gatherings for differences in philosophy. God can have you build with people with different opinions to adequately build you by showing you your blind spots so you can be used for more honorable work.

There are many things to watch out for, that can assure you that you are still a lively stone:

1) Flexibility to the move of the Holy Spirit. John 3:8 says, "The wind blows where it listeth, and thou heareth the sound thereof, but cannot tell where it cometh and whither it goeth: so is everyone that is born of the Spirit." Lively stones are ready for the move of the Spirit and ready to follow the frequency of the

spirit. Elijah was a man of the Spirit. He needed a ride from the mount of the contest with the prophets of Baal. He got a ride in the realm of the Spirit and got to the gate of Jezreel before King Ahab (1 Kings 18:46).

2) Usefulness for Special purposes. 2 Timothy. 2:20-22 says, "But in a great house there are not only vessels of gold and of silver, but also of wood and of earth; and some to honor and some to dishonor. If a man therefore purges himself from these, he shall be a vessel unto honor, sanctified, and meet for the master's use and prepared unto every good work." Lively stones are special vessels that are used for the honorable mission because you have what it takes to represent His interest.

3) Divine inspiration. Job. 32:8 says, "There is a Spirit in man and the inspiration of God almighty gives that spirit understanding." Lively stones are specially endowed with unusual inspiration to be ahead of his equals. Lively stones are pacesetters, they never run out of ideas that bring glory to God.

4) Result-oriented. Isaiah 48:17 says, "Thus saith the Lord, thy Redeemer, the Holy one of Israel, I am the Lord thy God which teacheth thee to profit, which leadeth thee by the way that thou shouldest go." Lively stones are result-oriented. God's special hand is on them for profitability for the kingdom of God and the demonstration of how much God can use those that yield to Him as a showpiece for His glory.

5) Fire in the Bones. Psalm 104:4 says, "Who maketh his angels spirits, his ministers a flaming fire." Lively stones carry the power that is needed to pull down stubborn strongholds to easily fulfill God's mandate for their lives.

In addition to the indications above, lively stones are special vessels needed to offer spiritual sacrifices acceptable to God. The spiritual sacrifices include the following:

Praise: Hebrews 13:15, Ps 67:5-6.

Good works: Hebrews 13:16.

Christian Converts: Roans. 15:15-16.

Financial Giving: Acts 10: 4, 31, Philippians 4:18.

Prayer: Revalations 8:3-4.

Any wonder why people request prayer from you? Unknowingly to you, and they can see the hand of God upon your life, they have faith in your prayer life that you can offer an acceptable sacrifice to God through prayers. This reality shows that you are a lively stone.

Some years ago, I worked in a school as a teacher where one of the students came to me to confess that he was a wizard and had some sort of power to do anyone that offends him harm. Immediately, I took him to the proprietor who happens to be a Pastor and narrated the story to him. He immediately pleaded with me to take the student away and pray over him. I was surprised and amazed at the same time. I did what he asked me to do and was never afraid of any repercussions because I believed I was a lively stone, positioned to offer spiritual sacrifices including praying for and over people as occasion demands.

You may find yourself in overwhelming situations that demand more than you can bear. Do not think you do not have enough to offer for we all have something to render. As lively stones, we have been positioned to make an impact on other people's lives.

Don't hold back when God is expecting you to express yourself in one area or the other. If the widow of Zaraphet had hoarded her flour from Elijah, maybe she and her son would have eaten their last meal and truly died as she asserted (1 Kings 17: 12). However, she believed in the man of God, and she never experienced lack afterward. God knew the widow had little, yet He sent Elijah to the widow, and it was left for her to build for God irrespective of her lack or condition. Don't allow your condition to stop you from being a lively stone, you can be passing up an opportunity to be announced.

Going through a tough time like Joseph is not always an indication that you are under demonic attack or are not needed to offer spiritual sacrifices acceptable to God, but maybe a process to prepare you for a greater task. Joseph had an assurance for a great future yet, his route to greatness was not a pleasant one. He was confronted (many times) to engage as a lively stone even as a slave and he never disappointed God. His testimony was, "how can I do this great wickedness and sin again God" (Genesis 39:9).

Even after his season of trial, his season of abundance was lived as a lively stone. Joseph had a good testimony even under pressure. In Genesis 50:20, he said, "You intended to harm me, but God intended it all for good. He brought me to this position so I could save the lives of many people." Like Joseph, God is still in search of believers who are true to their identity as lively stones in all of the life circumstances (good or bad). Many Christians use their conditions as an excuse for failures, but the truest test of time is choosing God even amid uncertainty. I once noticed a quote on my social media that said, "prosperity opens up the depth of arrogance that has been concealed over the years by suffering."

You learn the true nature of a man when he is under pressure, therefore, you can still be a lively stone even in your toughest moments. Christ has paid the price; you just have to be available for use and you will be like a city that is set on a hill that cannot be hidden. You are that City!

About The Author

Benard Obichie is a humble and passionate man of God with a penchant for raising mature believers and restoring the integrity of the body of Christ. He is highly gifted in the areas of preaching, teaching, healing, and counseling. He leads a parish of The Redeemed Christian Church of God, Fountain of Restoration Parish in Buffalo, New York. He is happily married to Pastor (Mrs) Dorothy Obichie and they are blessed with three beautiful children (Light, Fruitful, and Crown of Glory).